systems for the future of feeling

Also by Kimberly Grey

The Opposite of Light

systems for the future of feeling

poems

kimberly grey

A Karen & Michael Braziller Book

PERSEA BOOKS / NEW YORK

Persea Books, Inc.
90 Broad Street
New York, New York 10004

Library of Congress Cataloging-in-Publication Data

Names: Grey, Kimberly, 1985– author.
Title: Systems for the future of feeling : poems / Kimberly Grey.
Description: First. | New York, New York : Persea Books, [2020] | Includes bibliographical references. | Summary: "These inventive and agonizing poems look, in heartbreaking paradox, to language to explore its effort and inadequacies, as they grapple with disintegrating love and surging terror in modern society. Urgently, Kimberly Grey explores the need for empathy and consolation-our desire (and responsibility) as beings in the world to express the inexpressible, comprehend the incomprehensible, bear the unbearable. Communing throughout with literary forebearers-Anne Carson, Jack Gilbert, Sina Queyras Gertrude Stein-Grey looks to build "language systems" in order to help us create relevant expressions for expressing awe, confusion, bewilderment, nostalgia, horror, and joy"—Provided by publisher.
Identifiers: LCCN 2020009313 | ISBN 9780892555208 (paperback : acid-free paper)
Subjects: LCGFT: Poetry.
Classification: LCC PS3607.R49935 S97 2020 | DDC 811/.6—dc23
LC record available at https://lccn.loc.gov/2020009313

Book design and composition by Rita Lascaro
Typeset in Adobe Garamond Pro
Manufactured in the United States of America. Printed on acid-free paper.

for myself and strangers

Contents

Rhetoric

If language formed a center.
If the center were true and tugging.
If the tugging kinged us and we were fully assembled.
If we were translated into compasses and the wind spun us around.
If the ground imagined us raveled.

If we strung milkweed around our shoulders and walked north.
If we found a little house and labeled it *covet*.
If it were contemptible to be personal and diamondly lit.

If we bathed.
If the neighbors watched us bathe.
If we knew our way around a waist and an equation.

If dirty were a symptom of wonder.

If we were dirty with wonder.

If we slapped a tender star and remembered our god.

If remembering is always suffering.
If there was a term for suffering in thought.
If thought were radioactive and red.

If we wandered through a gallery of horse tails.
If we thought it was modern architecture.
If the mechanics of thought were the mechanics of architecture.
If we could build thinking with a chisel and hair.

If we are scared to let go of our hotness.
If hotness is a menial term.
If hotness had anything to do with the equation.
If our bodies were a hundred lying birds.
If our bodies were disassembled.

If we are failing.
If failing is gathered in the mind.
If we mind failing.
If we leap from place to place and never arrive.

If we are unkinged.
If we suffer for language and a little house.
If truth is contemptible and wonder is a symptom of god.
If we build god with a compass and bath.
If the neighbors watch and wonder.

If language equals failure and failure is the end.
If we disassemble the center.
If we wander back to where we arrived.

If the ground is a gallery of horse tails.
If we bury our failures in the ground.
If we wait for them to bloom.
If a horse comes and pisses on them

can we be happy still?

*

System of Knowing

Everything I remember of anything starts with a name, the strange
sound of it, before that little opening that splinters a thing into knowing—

how precisely the weather calls us "hers" when she has nothing else to name
and our little houses are quivered into piles. It hurts, even when we don't know

why or what to call it. Now a neighbor can sit on the toilet and see
straight through to the sky and maybe we can't call this *actual ruin*
because there is a man in Sing Sing with no sky. He will never have a sky
again because he killed a woman whose name he didn't know.

What's his name? Why don't we know

it? We are terrestrial and bigness is our fascination. A man is just one
man. There is a crisis in scale when you don't understand it. There is
a poverty of the mind and if you don't know

what it is, you suffer from it. It's akin to *Ein Wehn im Gott. Ein Wind.* It sweeps
through our heads as wind through wildflowers. It never sticks. For too long
now I've been spoiled by what I don't know.

I've left sections of a face untouched. I've gripped the sides of a moving train
without grasping the historical context. I've studied the architecture of
a fence—the violent kind of architecture that is only intelligible
to those kept inside it. The soul is a pain I know

I don't know.

I've had the privilege of dashing away from a lover who was dangerously
backlit. Everything I can remember about his body is museumed
in an immaculately distanced placed. The privilege of knowing

him alive and only alive. To not imagine him any other way.
When it's evening, when the tall green world sprouts into the sky as if to say *I know*

why I'm here, we don't completely understand it. We are not beings who know

a thing from a thing except by the names we call them. It's why I wandered
for days through a beech tree forest and not once thought of Klimt's *Buchenwald*
but only of Buchenwald. No,

death is never small, but sometimes it's not large. Sometimes it's the size
of a leaf stuck to the bottom of your shoe, its symmetry
veined with a history you still don't know

could never know

and you are galloped by it. It's never enough, to be astonished.

Interview with Gertrude Stein

Why do you write?
GS: "I am writing for myself and strangers. This is the only way that I can do it. Everybody is a real one to me, everybody is like some one else too to me. No one of them that I know can want to know it and so I write for myself and strangers." (*The Making of Americans*)

Why do you repeat the way you do?
GS: "There is then always repeating in all living." (*The Making of Americans*)

How are repetition and memory linked?
GS: "There is no left or right without remembering. And remembering." (*Identity A Poem*)

It seems you really love language.
GS: "I like the feeling of words doing as they want to do and as they have to do when they live where they have to live that is where they have come to live which of course they do do." (*Lecture I*)

Do you feel misunderstood?
GS: "How pleasantly I feel contented with that." (*An Elucidation*)

I've heard you like food? What's your favorite dish?
GS: "Apple plum, carpet steak, seed clam, colored wine, calm seen, cold cream, best shake, potato, potato and no no gold work with pet, a green seen is called bake and change sweet is bready, a little piece, a little piece a little piece please." (*Tender Buttons*)

Are you sure you're talking about food?
GS: "Very pleasant weather we are having." (*Bon Marche Weather*)

Alright I'll be more general.
GS: "The teasing is tender and trying and thoughtful." (*Tender Buttons*)

What is love?
GS: "Love of a person makes better soften." (*History or Messages from History*)

What is loss?
GS: "A widow in a wise veil and more garments shows that shadows are even." (*Tender Buttons*)

What is fear?
GS: "A dark grey, a very dark grey, a quite dark grey is monstrous ordinarily, it is so monstrous because there is no red in it." (*Tender Buttons*)

What is life?
GS: "Elephant beaten with candy and little pops and chews all bolts and reckless reckless rats, this is this." (*Tender Buttons*)

What is language?
GS: "Sentences are historical." (*We Came. A History*)

What is repetition?
GS: "Sometimes it is very hard to understand the meaning of repeating." (*The Making of Americans*)

Try.
GS: "A language tires. A language tries to be. A language tries to be free." (*Photograph*)

We Were Civilized When?

Remember when we were not in sadness as in a bomb-hole? (The science
of us analyzed like that, proved our long deepenings). How long
has it been since we've endlessly felt human? (answer this, endlessly).
In Rome, the ancient ruins look like ruins. We swarm them, (no,
not touching) all the broken things that last. Though we rarely mention
it: how modernly ruined we are. It is a characteristic of a system to speak
of its working, of its interacting parts, of the whole, complex thing.
But pain has uninvented us. Anthropologists rested on the idea
that one day we'd function. Everything's a fiction. What's beautiful
is principal now (even if not real): Roman cathedrals, hotel gardens,
five colors of sky. I'm not supposed to be here; this country is not mine.
Yet I am singed red for its arrangement. I want your saddest statue
parts on my lap: spine and wrist and head. I want you not-hard, not
ever dead. *Dai retta, dai retta* (feel it in the lung). Something foreign
is knitting the hurt inside us up and look: how softly out we come.

Proper Expressions of Love

accident   we find ourselves living

roles   as acrobats
           in a house

scene   the telephone rings
           we twist
           our wrists

pattern   our backsides lift,
           become jeweled
           with shadows

judgment   it is beautiful

reality   disguise is in everything
           (even language)

articulations   *every day*
           I don't
           remember
           I love you
           I dig you

metaphor   a happy grave

uncertainty   I don't know
           how to save you, which
           way to go, how to live

certainty   without any doubt, but

future   right *now*, *now*, and *now*

transference   your lungs make me
           in make me out

System of Becoming Quite

You have memorable hair, you own property
in Munich, which explains your longish need
to be so distantly lit. I used to know your anguish
like the body of a fat fish I ate and ate it.
It is good to make a large thing rompish
inside you. When we were young, once,
we were happyish people, we were
unrecognizable in our smallish folds. It was
a pretty way to start. There are thousands
of atmospheres to try. If you beam you are
almost beaming. If it is brutal, then brutalish
is a way to live. Lovers never sufficiently love
anything. It's a wildish thing. It has always
astonished me, the way they are boundary with
their haves and half-wits. The way they claim
fantastically to know you from the darkish start.
Everything is becoming quite and not not.
Out here, a bridge is our god. We praise it
in a highish way. When I want you to stay
I tell you Munich is damn far away and we
have all this goldish light to contain. You are
becoming the considerable extent to which
I extend to. We are almost there. I'd happily
teach you a newish way to be here. Or on
your saddening days, dismantle your beautiful
ish-ness and carry it utterly away.

Simultaneously

I am and you are, as larks going, at the same time, away and up, unthought of separately, a blurred black-thing against blue, though we are different, and two. And soon we'll be lost to a chasm. While moving is an immense gesture, it almost means we can, as astonishingly as things change, be the same. You will understand,

*

As your plane lands here, didn't the lady once say in the event of aloneness please hold on? Why have you gone? Here is a question I've tried: why at the same time as speaking are we moving away? Though the theory of action explains it well, the function of experience must be experimental. And, too, I knew assuredly that

*

Once, while slow and desperate, we behaved almost as a low wind, no shame or control. We were as simple as photographs, rendered images, at the same time as living with our figures and it figures you so besieged me that I decided to live, while also sad, in your sadness. Yes, I'll wear that black dress

*

When I meet you at the gate, you'll be walking and I'll be walking and we'll both know things cut across time, and how lucky that no time is lost, those small repeated reliefs. Time deserves to be studied, as I study you and me and how we are linked. See we've become almost like holy things, while the reverse is also true and every time I see you, while I'm looking,

*

I'm thinking of a long river, something with no end, as a real river somewhere does, at the same time, into a true-blue sky. It is the same way I imagine us ending, like two parts of the same broken line, who go down trying, as the planes are flying, as the dying are dying, as the not dying are dying, as lovers and lover, I've figured it out: you are only mine when you are moved, at the same time, the same way, I'm moved.

If You Are Running

Be sure that love is not a large stampede.

Be sure that love is a small one.

A Difficult System

I love a man who is difficult to love, the way a horse is difficult to ride
when the horse is a man. Or when you don't stroke him enough, or you
do, but you stroke him wrongly and you don't love him completely.

I love the difficulty of loving a man incompletely. His blue, his black,
his back, I have not mounted enough, it's hard. The body is difficult,
even the horse's body, its muscled frame

always galloping away. Its mane, the main reason, I mean, is to stay,
to hold on, they're hard to know the difference between. I could say
that loving a man is an easy task. I could say the man and I are
beautiful like two horses

in the earliest, blurry light. Always love is useless. Or the horse is
because you don't know how to ride it and it can't run fast enough
or it runs too fast and there you are standing alone
in a field as it rushes

past you. Let's not mistake what's difficult here: the man, the manner
of loving him or leaving him. Or believing him, that his body wants
to be had easily by your body and not by any body
that can be simply had.

I love a man who is difficult to love, the way a man is difficult to love,
the way a horse that is running keeps on running so you will hold it
harder. So hold it harder, its continuously difficult body, then go on
loving him, easily, as hard.

Proper Expressions of Desire

thought   Desire is not a thing

thought   I can give up
                           easily

System with Some Truth

It's valuable when swimming to know you're swimming
        it's true
in hurried movements we are most ourselves. Once a person
asked if we are valuable to each other, I said *that's personal.*
        It's truly
smart to answer personal questions in a hurried manner.
Once I couldn't
find any real beauty in you to last. Our bodies are
        true variety.
Our bodies are
        what's true
of maps—too many rivers to drown in. In Dubrovnik,
there's one of the smallest rivers in the world. We'd drown in it.
A river never rests. It's a personal choice to rest. After a long time
moving we speak about resting, we speak and it's
        true, language
never rests. *I'm actually tired. Actually, I'm tired.* This is
        a true fact.
We are not exactly beautiful and *what is beautiful* is
a personal question. Yes
        it's true, you are
the accumulation of losing which means I am
lost. In a river, everything is lost in the hurrying; the rocks,
the fish. I wish it were kept
personal, the losing. I have considered our bodies' need to keep
moving, through states, through
        true statements.
It's valuable to know language
will not make us beautiful. It's valuable to watch a body
swimming in a river that isn't yours. A river is not
        the reason
we cannot help ourselves. Water only kind of
drowns us and the rest we do ourselves. I am tired
of your kind of
        beauty,
that moves and keeps on moving. I am
the kind of fish you are losing.

Prepositions Against Desire

Across the bed, separately, like Phoenician fighters, like lovers and even more unraveling,
a system of two, for three days, four.

*

It could be over, I think, every time we make it here. Such twinfish, there's something
like an electrification. But we are many things. There are many seas, fish, in   them.

*

Before we read Longus (*all lovers believe they are inventing love*) we believed we invented it.

*

We are radical on the inside, our minds revolutionized the idea of touching
by not touching. We grab each other

                             only at the metaphorical root.

*

Besides   what's refusal, what's a moan, a yes, no
              please, go, rush now. Slow. And as if with a soft brush
              an ancient writer strokes us
              into letters, forked lines, fine,
              with a hand that

*

                        don't stop.

*

Language is the body our bodies ogle over. Language is the ultimate hobby.

*

We are theoretically between here and there. We are theoretical boundaries. From
the outside we might resemble theories of lovers contradicting theories of lovers.

           *

Those theories being: into difficulty, we must go.

                      *

Since we were once over. As we speak, we construct time, which is also a construct that has constructed us.

*

Underneath the covers, the light animates us. Essentially, we are the movement that animates us. Fundamentally, we are the dark that animates the light that animates us.

             *

There's too much space in the possibility of space. Movement is something beyond language. We are moving   see us   moving across

       *

with, within, without.

System for After

Even, happenstance.
Even if we were differently young.
Even at home, after the reaching, the glance.
Even after we were in the business of after.
Even when it's heavy and hurts.
Even when we could pair it with now.
Even if there was a boat I could take back to you.
Even if the hothouse resembles the world in its inability to calm down:
      Licht Licht Licht.
Even enough of it now. How do you say bursting in every language?
Even I don't know it.
Even if we love memory.
Even if we use it as a way to devotion.
The future hasn't happened yet but still it is happening.
Even when it tries not to.
Curiosity happens faster.
Devotion is a cricket's song. Even when it's not.
Even when we dragged it around like a block of light just to see if it lasted.
Even when it breaks.
Even when we know it will break.
Let's be shocked, after.

Interview with Sina Queyras

Is technology hurting us?
SQ: "How good we have become at hashtags, and how distanced from our bodies, I walk in mine so surprised to feel anything." (*M X T*)

Are we beyond needing the comfort of each other?
SQ: "Such lovely company your memory is, and on the train today a sweet man from Turkey upright as a maypole." (*M X T*)

But what about present, human bodies?
SQ: "Listen there was a time. Listen we all knew. Listen it was so fast." (*Lemon Hound*)

How about the disparity between men and women?
SQ: "The women plug themselves in. They work hard. They untwist bread bags and dole out dabs of butter. They choose low-fat milk. They have bought digital cameras. They join food co-ops. They find recycling sources. They mail things diligently. They see the sun as unlimited potential." (*Lemon Hound*)

Does that mean it's harder to be a woman?
SQ: "She is calling home, Calling the past, calling out for anyone To hear." (*Expressway*)

What do you wish women would hear?
SQ: "I don't know. I am thinking of something about breasts. There is a relationship between water and the breast. Did you know that the breast is water? There is water in a breast. My breasts, I mean, they aren't idle." (*M X T*)

So how does a woman move?
SQ: "I love the old questions." (*M X T*)

Do you want to ask the questions?
SQ: "The endless loop of feeling, what does it reveal?" (*M X T*)

Maybe it reveals the truth.
SQ: "But what is truth. Fact? Body? Idea? Word?" (*Expressway*)

I think you know better than I do.
SQ: "You swim into splendidness. I will follow you there." (*M X T*)

And what if you get there first?
SQ: "I wish you luck. I think of your future, after I am gone. I assume you will have one."
(*M X T*)

Why wouldn't I?
SQ: "It takes so long to say anything. I haven't time to be optimistic." (*M X T*)

If you had to be optimistic for both of us, what would the future look like?
SQ: "We become missiles hurled against the city. We mix with unknown quantities. We covet and dive. We come together and split off. We are never sure who we are without others. We marry. We grope in the dark." (*Lemon Hound*)

Proper Expressions of Sadness

shape	all loss is rectangle (all love too)
verbs	it hurts to stuff it in, to pry it out, to hold it down, it is
size & weight	so large so gold and
possession	my, my, mine
length	I've known it as long as knowledge, as long as
color	blue has existed
tense	see, once you knew, then you know,
consistency	its soggy drooped blossoms, though
sequence	you'll see it standing there in first and last order
appearance	trying to be upright
direction	all this way and that way
arrangement	like flowered string lights all strung I am one
shade	light that is
desire	burned out or wants to be
thought	fastidiously

If You Are Pining

No way to hold you and so
I do what the pines do:
not be trees but be full
of want and waiting
and detachment, dement—
I so wish to de-miss you.

The Mercy of Pronouns

The large difficulty of mercy is that it's full of people

moving and sometimes you are not one of them.

I say this to him. What I mean is there's no interpretable

order, no structure, no owner. No one, holding a flower,

you can predict at your door. I want him to feel

as I feel, which, right away, is ambiguous.

Sometimes a *you* is a lover, but he is not my lover.

He is a man looking at me asking about mercy.

Every time I say *you,* I imagine a curtain between us

rising. Now when I say *him*, it closes back down.

Mercy is many things I don't say. His wife indelibly

at home, cutting the carrots down raw for him, the soup

she simmers on their stove, our shivering. Every time

I look away from him, I mean to (as I am not doing now).

Mercy is knowing (holding) the difference (the distance).

Interview with Anne Carson

I hope you don't mind if I ask some personal questions?
AC: "My personal poetry is a failure." (*Decreation*)

Alright, then maybe you can answer some of my personal questions?
AC: "Do you fear the same things as I fear?" (*Men in the Off Hours*)

Probably. Let's see.
AC: "Yes I admit a degree of unease about my motives in making this documentary." (*Men in the Off Hours*)

What's the point of loving others?
AC: "There is a black planet speeding towards us." (*Glass, Irony and God*)

Why is the sky so insistent?
AC: "Existence will not stop until it gets to beauty…" (*The Beauty of the Husband*)

Why did my mother leave my father?
AC: "A wife is in the grip of being." (*The Beauty of the Husband*)

Why did their marriage fail?
AC: "…if it is a game, if they know the rules, and it was and they did." (*The Beauty of the Husband*)

Why does life hurt so much, even when we expect it?
AC: "The tough wound plucks itself." (*Decreation*)

And why can't I sleep?
AC: "What could be more hopeful than this story of an empty eye filled with seeing as it sleeps?" (*Decreation*)

To move forward, what must I leave behind?
AC: "Love dares the self to leave itself behind, to enter into poverty." (*Decreation*)

Is that why life feels so hard?
AC: "It takes practice to shave the skin off the light." (*Men in the Off Hours*)

What do we do when love is ending?

AC: "Life pulls softly inside your bindings. The pod glows—dear stench." (*Men in the Off Hours*)

And how do I get to the other side?

AC: "The actions of life are not so many. To go in, to go, to go in secret, to cross the Bridge of Sighs." (*Short Talks*)

And the difference between love and grief?

AC: "Well you know I wonder, it could be love running towards my life with its arms up yelling let's buy it what a bargain!" (*Short Talks*)

If You Need Meaning

In the ever-morning, meaning
is determined by light. It is ever.
The meaning. Meaning you
have a lifetime to figure it out.
When the light's out. Or
when the ever is

out of the light.

Proper Expressions of Pain

sound	cutting the blue sky in two as a trumpet a trumpet is building like
action	a magical divagation
appetite	devouring a form of star points
nouns	so many stones
people	a lover, a bad lover, a gone lover once told me without saying
pronouns	he told me, he said, *you are*
absolute phrase	*not necessary*
fragment	*no good lover,* I am
movement	like Etel said: "a woman in whose brain trains [are] whistling"
image	through every darkgreen forest darkly
faith	believe it, every loss, every time is a phenomenon
phenomenon	the sea coming out of the sea leaving the sea

Interview with Jack Gilbert

Tell me, what is language for?
JG: "A place to stand. To receive. A place to go into from." (*Views from Jeopardy*)

Was it constructed just for human beings?
JG: "The horse wades in the city of grammar." (*Views from Jeopardy*)

So we are more alike than we think, humans and animals?
JG: "You know I am serious about the whales." (*Views from Jeopardy*)

What about people?
JG: "Watching my wife out in the full moon, the sea bright behind her across the field and through the trees. Eight years and her love for me quieted away. How fine she is. How hard we struggle." (*Monolithos*)

Aren't all marriages a struggle?
JG: "It is hard to understand how we could be brought here by love." (*Monolithos*)

What can we understand?
JG: "Things that are themselves. Waves water, the rocks stone. The smell of her arms. Stillness. Windstorms. The long silence again. The well. The rabbit. Heat." (*Monolithos*)

What do you mean by the long silence?
JG: "What we are busy with doesn't make us groan . . ." (*Monolithos*)

What are you currently busy with?
JG: "Not wanting to lose it all for poetry." (*Monolithos*)

Why? Is poetry ineffective?
JG: "How astonishing is it that language can almost mean, and frightening that it does not quite. *Love*, we say, *God*, we say, *Rome* and *Michiko*, we write, and the words get it wrong. We say *bread* and it means according to which nation. French has no word for home, and we have no word for strict pleasure." (*The Great Fires*)

What gives you pleasure?
JG:"The man does not want to know rapture by standing outside himself. He wants to know delight as the native land he is." (*The Great Fires*)

So pleasure is already within us?
JG: "Not as pleasure but a way to get to something darker." (*Refusing Heaven*)

I feel like the tone has changed.
JG: "The Greek fishermen do not play on the beach and I don't write funny poems."
(*Refusing Heaven*)

What's the darkest thing you've written?
JG: "I was lying on the deck with my eyes closed . . ." (*Refusing Heaven*)

Very funny. I really want to know.
JG: "If there was water once, there isn't now. Rock and hammering sun. He tastes all of it
again and again, his madeleine." (*The Dance Most of All*)

I think you can do better. There's a lot of light in there.
JG: "People complain about too many moons in my poetry." (*The Dance Most of All*)

*What about: "I lie in the dark wondering if this quiet in me now is a beginning or an end." (The
Dance Most of All)*
JG: "To tell you instead of my private life among people who must wrestle their hearts in
order to feel anything, as though it were unnatural. What I master by day still lapses at night.
But I go on, with the cargo cult, blindly feeling the snow come down, learning to flower by
tightening." (*Monoliths*)

A System of Holding

If there's a horse in the mindfield, if there's more than one horse,
       hold them,
as to not rush them, as to not rush away from the violence
of staying. There are two ways to
       hold people—
one is by grief. The other is by the physics with which you know
them—a bedfellow's arms swaddled and tugged around you means you have
       held him
hardly enough. I said bedfellow, not lover, because so far this could be
any century. Hektor did not approve of war. Who is Hektor? He means
       "to hold" you.
I'll *Hektor* you, he *Hektored* down that job, she *Hektored* back
from joy. This is all
       so old.
Just say it: when you love someone, you are consenting to the grief that comes
with loving them. We are objects affected by the light exploration of hands.
I was ravished by a man
       for a whole
year. I knew him sufficiently and geometrically. His body fit into mine
so much that we were sucking and bordered and building.
       I held
him, and all his horses, as the TV shook with planes. If there was a day we all
       wished to hold
each other it would have been that day. Look, people are captivating
in loss, as long as we are not them. As long as the ones we
       want to hold
are not excruciatingly dead. So many of us were
       holding each other
the night before, how different things could've been; if that morning
the country was collected by the neck of its throes, and together
we screamed we all just screamed
       don't go

Postmodern Dirge

It is voluntary to love each other
now. Because we have not

grown more simple. Because
in our dreams it always replays,

the day the planes were flying
and then not flying. The buildings

standing and then gone. I think
we should have a new kind of dreaming

where planes transform into women
where women transform

into buildings and the men inside them
jump and the women transform

into a soft sea below. Because it is still so
unimaginable—the act of jumping,

the fact of buildings and people
high in them and no sea. And men

who loved women and men who loved
men and children

who loved their fathers and
mothers who jumped too.

What we need now is a bed
smoothed into the side of a mountain

where we could sleep. How beautiful
the nerve of us to think

we have plenty of time and breathing.

If You Are Suffering

Look at the knees,
the knots of the body—

just roll up your jeans to see.

Family System

That we are eased often, into, and from each other means
we have options. Like the body easily deciding
when it loves and when it unloves, an estuary of sorts.
It becomes source-like,
where all things run. It's so much like that. Anyone
who has a body knows, perhaps it's for geographical reasons,
we go (and it's rampant) toward
the thing that unwants us. In fact, I demonstrated it. Once
in a house where nothing loved
me I loved everything back. It was astonishing.
The furniture curled against backbones
and those people didn't know, those people
didn't know what to do. So together
we suffered with a yellowing ease. Even the trees outside were
quiet. I estimate that's all it took, a day,
maybe longer—to become like an erasure. They erased me
from that house, held the curtains open
wider, until the light unshaped my love (not shock-
ingly) into something harder.

Love in the Time of Formlessness
(or Form in the Time of Lovelessness)

We need a form to form us, we need a form to teach
us the facts. How, actually, it is form that un-renders us
now: my back against your back.

This is experimental. We need a form to re-form us.
Your face and my face are just shapes, cracked
and stacked like blue cubes,

like two single wounds. What is time, I mean, what
is time? Are we, in order to be kept, too keeping?
Is love really a mountain

that just stops? When I say, *why aren't you weeping*
I mean, *weep with me.* We need an affectionate form,
we need a home various

with love. This is experimental. Everything is sad
but I cannot describe the sad. I can only describe
the outside of sadness

which is like a slug and too soft to touch or take.
Are we alright in each other and is form just a question
of what we can't make?

We need a form that informs us. Everything is
wrecked, our house is wrecking, we have stumbled
out of, wherefrom, near

to and hence—even language has become
useless and bent; we no longer know
where the word *love* has went.

Consoling System

There are a million griefs flying out there the president says
        we have unthinkable hugeness
    arms to hold us—
they're not suffering exactly but suffering exactly and it's hard
        to distinguish a zero from
    an egg but
there is only one that's breakable—we are the ones with neckbones
        we are absolutely beginning
    to understand that
there is no one ancient wail they are all immense and the president
        should not dare to stop
    our wishing
there was an end or at least a slower wound or a grocery store
        that would give us some food—
    and everywhere
there are people waiting to die people waiting for us to vote so
        they can be president and die
    one day too
their whole lives more important because they are more important
        because they tell us
    don't worry
there are greater tragedies than you—the president says there is
        no orthodox way to hold something dying
    you must be
there to let it shock you until you are all smashed and gold and flickering
        with hurt—look out
    the window
there is sun and half of a large sea and the president is telling us we all
        have extravagant faces
    but he isn't telling us
there are mistakes that he has made and whatever lastness he creates
        will be ours—we will have it
    to carry on
there and everywhere on our backs east and westly and afterwards (if there
        are afterwords) we'll realize
    we never really knew

there was a way to say sorry without saying it—without giving anything away
        how is it that we are
    always waiting
there like forget-me-nots waiting for our blueness to be picked—
        how does a president con
    how does he soul and where—
there by the building's last wishbone—there by the rapacious bouquet of bodies—
        there by the towers
    of sad geniuses—
there by the darkness made famous for being darkness—for being one last
        wreckage to love but where
    there there.

Proper Expressions of Depression

wish

you want nothing but

image

to understand the figure
that represents the idea

clarity

for sense to match sensation
because

problem

it's impossible to love
what you can't feel

origin

it began in a place
of unknowing
and then became unknown

translation

there is less language
now and no
decipherable meaning

imagination

like Adrienne said: "the failure
of imagination"

cost

everything

diameter

is growing, though
the growing
is shrinking, it's difficult

realm

the mind is in one

season

perpetual winter and

sequence

syntax can't
reorder the world

ambition

you want / the word
to see / the symbol
but

picture

tree is not a tree

Unsystem the System

We don't say *we are armed* when we mean our arms.
We don't say we are armed,
       though our arms are real,
they are really arms, we could use them
to disarm ourselves now.
       We could use them
       to squeeze or hold or load
          not a gun, not a gun,
    please not another gun.
But maybe a face that needs holding,
       or some laundry
       that needs folding. Like that other night
         when I faced you, pulled your shirt
       over your arms and heard you say,
       everyone deserves this.
And I didn't know if you meant a shirt
or arms or just someone
       to pull it off of you.
         Someone to touch
       your free skin, to see the face
when a shirt leaves it, in good awe.
Awe which sounds like
       Arms. Arms that could be,
         are they, sometimes, just, only, these
blasted and beautiful extensions—
Lover I've said so much. World we have not said. No
       we don't say *armed*
       when we mean *our arms,*
though we are armed. Though we are, all
       of us, perfectly armed.

If You Need Reminding

knees
moss
distance
a perfect listener
experiments
disguises
digging
eggs
singing
the nakedness of
winter
arriving with rain
mountains
wounds
locks
circles of
soft feet
marriage
new fire
butcher shops
brushstrokes
eyelids
scaffolds
filings of silver
slivers of bone
smoke
star systems
low fevers
airplanes
long distances
noon
wounds
glancing out
slow blue
sound
the sound of
howling

finally leaving
a palace of
expectance
nerves
a small hotel
a hilltop
gold fog
apples
the smell of light
pinnacles
a fistful of flowers
entangling
lonely animals
horizon
another's face
sudden humor
another's face
hammering
no warning
old rooms
wounds
the head of a pin
proportions
blushing
islands
half a thought
fastening onto
breathing into
medium cathedrals
no shadow
blood or desire
midspring
pulling
opening
one's clothes
ancient trees
a beautiful scroll

pleasure
a photograph of
a lover
coming
secret names
cheekbones
wounds
a little ash
age
nests
birds whipping
a loud river
good translation
canyons
back roads
the entire truth of
almost monuments of
language
approaching

Interview with Ludwig Wittgenstein

Is it possible to fully arrive at meaning?
LW: "Here meaning gets imagined as a kind of mental pointing, indicating." (*Zettel 3e*)

So it's all a matter of directives?
LW: "Can you order someone to understand a sentence? Why can't one tell someone: 'Understand that!' Couldn't I obey the order 'Understand this Greek sentence by learning Greek?'— Similarly: one can say 'Produce pain in yourself', but not 'Have pain'". (*Zettel 11e*)

Does that mean we are always failing?
LW: "Like everything metaphysical the harmony between thought and reality is to be found in the grammar of the language." (*Zettel 12e*)

So meaning is possible?
LW: "Some sentences have to be read several times to be understood as sentences." (*Zettel 15e*)

Is that why language is often inadequate?
LW: "I expect an explosion any moment." (*Zettel 11e*)

But I must understand that inadequacy.
LW: "Remember that our language might possess a variety of different words: one for 'thinking out loud'; one for thinking as one talks to oneself in the imagination; one for a pause during which something or other floats before the mind, after which, however, we are able to give a confident answer. One word for a thought expressed in a sentence; one for the lightning thought which I may later 'clothe in words'; one for wordless thinking as one works." (*Zettel 23e*)

So the availability of words opens a space for the possibility of thought?
LW: "Are roses red in the dark?—One can think of the rose in the dark as red.—" (*Zettel 47e*)

You have more questions than answers.
LW: "Isn't flame mysterious because it is impalpable? All right—but why does that make it mysterious? Why should something impalpable be more mysterious than something palpable? Unless it's because we *want* to catch hold of it." (*Zettel 23e*)

What's wrong with wanting to grasp something?
LW: "How words are understood is not told by words alone." (*26e*)

Give me an example.

LW: "Has the verb 'to dream' a present tense? How does a person learn to use this?" (*72e*)

I don't know. You tell me.

LW: "Why do you demand explanations? If they are given to you, you will once more be facing a terminus. They cannot get you any further than you are at present." (*58e*)

I'm just tired of all the sadness.

LW: "Suppose it were said: 'Gladness is a feeling, and sadness consists in *not* being glad'. —Is the absence of a feeling a feeling?" (*Zettel 90e*)

I don't think feeling allows for an absence.

LW: "The concept of pain is characterized by its particular function in our life." (*Zettel 94e*)

So there is a system for meaning?

LW: "In this case one might say: 'Only in the system has the sign any life'." (*26e*)

I just want to find a language we all won't suffer for.

LW: "Our motto might be: 'Let us not be bewitched'." (*119e*)

System with Some Memory

History is what the light keeps
is a definition of light. I wrote
it so you'd remember

*

the imaginary tools of love:
historical artifacts, hunt
together, bedsheets over
thighs, no plane departing
west of you, all the while

*

remembering it is happiness
not to. It is happiness
that composed of us a zero,

*

I wrote, because from memory
we'll be taken,

*

our history is what keeps
the light. Substitute *shame*
for *history*: read, one who stabs
at the world, one who is violent

*

in love, it is us, always,
repeating the past, a game
of dismembering

*

while remembering it is
happiness not to.

How We Take Our Grief

We take our grief privately and in the morning.
And drink our coffee and drink our tea.
We hold the newspaper out with our arms
and we hold the fork that holds the egg that holds
hunger. We put it in our mouth. We put it
in our mouth. Twice the clock strikes three
and privately we sit together. We think
the orange juice is too bright. We pour it
in a glass and think. We drink the brightness
and it disappears. We take the last muffin
and split it into three.
            Our two mouths hold each other.
Privately, we think it's the mind that holds us.
We sit striking the thought. We hold the clock
that holds the mind. We think the clock is
in our arms. We think the clock is our arms.
Privately, the thought disappears. We pour
the morning. We drink the morning together
and split the brightness. We take the morning
out of us and put it in our mouths. We drink
it. We hold our grief out in front of us.
We think this is private. We take our grief
and pour it in a glass. We think we have
mouths, we think we have arms to hold it.

Proper Expressions of Awe

position	centered in frame, it is necessary to look at
posture	the thing that is always up
age	and always new
question	is it good or bad
identification	that I (perpetually)
error	mistook it for beauty and found it
force	mauled my bones like a saint or bruise
endurance	do you know what it takes
disorder	to be that one thing constantly in a fit
speed	across time zones we are all
state	savage for it

No System for Grief

You were in the world and. More
slowly now I am

so fasted now so. Long
it's been without
you, if you ever read this
you were what. I was dreaming of

this welt, to know
it before. It comes like love
I loved your

empty spaces,

saved them a little
like. The sea
it's dying, believe me,
long ago today

I was. Fond of saying time is
just wandering away,

you heard me once say

I am the lost shiny thing

you were. Designed for
this decade, jumped hoops to get me

and picture it, got through
but not this I'm not through
and. I will not miss this big sadness or.

How I heard your body break into such.

Fragments toward what. Bewilder meant.

*

Reason

Because we are unbearable
Because in German *world* is *Welt*.
Because we discovered objects and infinity.
Because squares were homes we couldn't leave.

Because we ran forwardly toward the future.
Because the maps were gentle with us.
Because we sewed an island back together and lived on it for years.

Because we discovered lowliness in the garden.
Because it was a pretty rip in the earth.
Because we climbed to the rooftop and thought it could hold our weight.
Because the law says everything is in conflict.

Because the world is a violent object.
Because we slung along the plural of love in our jeans.
Because we knew it would be unbearable.

Because we discovered time and ran backwardly through the asters.
Because our homes were gentle and could hold our weight.
Because objects were empty and infinity, robust.

Because we consented to disgrace.
Because pain is connected to history and the world is lit up.
Because all law is thoughtless.

Because any day now we could be the lowliest in the garden.
Because we slung along the past in our jeans.
Because the plural of love is an island.

Because we couldn't leave.
Because we whispered *Welt, Welt.*
Because arranging the future is violence.

Notes

In "System of Knowing," the line "Ein Wehn im Gott. Ein Wind" is the last line of Sonnet #3 in Rainer Maria Rilke's *Sonnets to Orpheus*.

> Rilke, Rainer Maria. *Sonnets to Orpheus.* Translated by C.F. Macintyre. University of California Press,1964.

In "Proper Expressions of Pain," the line, "A woman in whose brain trains are whistling" is from Etel Adnan's poem "The XVI Return" in her book *To look at the sea is to become what one is*. I changed the verb tense.

> Adnan, Etel. *To look at the sea is to become what one is.* Volume II. Edited by Thom Donovon & Brandon Shimoda. Nightboat Books, 2014.

In "Proper Expressions of Depression," the line "the failure of imagination" is from Adrienne Rich's *What Is Found There: Notebooks on Poetry and Politics*. The entire quote reads, "Despair, when not the response to absolute physical and moral defeat, is, like war, the failure of imagination."

> Rich, Adrienne. *What Is Found There: Notebooks on Poetry and Politics.* W.W. Norton & Company, 2003.

In "Prepositions Against Desire," the line "All lovers believe they are inventing love" is from Anne Carson's essay "My Page Makes Love" in her book *Eros the bittersweet* in which she says of Longus' novel Daphnis and Chloe, "All lovers believe they are inventing love: Daphnis and Chloe actually *do* invent love."

> Carson, Anne. *Eros the bittersweet.* Dalkey Archive Press, 1998.

Lines from "Interview with Anne Carson" are from the following books:
> Carson, Anne. *Decreation:* Poetry, Essays, Opera. Vintage Books, 2005
> *Glass, Irony and God.* New Directions, 1992.
> *Men in the Off Hours.* Vintage Books, 2011.
> *Short Talks.* Brick Books, 1992.
> *The Beauty of the Husband: A Fictional Essay in 29 Tangos.* Vintage Books, 2001.

Lines from "Interview with Jack Gilbert" are from the following book:
> Gilbert, Jack. *Collected Poems.* Alfred A. Knopf, 2012.

Lines from "Interview with Sina Queyras" are from the following books:
> Queyras, Sina. *Expressway.* Toronto, Coach House Books, 2005.
> *Lemon Hound.* Toronto, Coach House Books, 2006.
> *M X T.* Toronto, Coach House Books, 2014.

Lines from "Interview with Gertrude Stein" are from the following book:
     Stein, Gertrude. *Selections*. Edited by Joan Retallack. University of California Press, 2008.

Lines from "Interview with Ludwig Wittgenstein" are from the following book:
     Wittgenstein, Ludwig. *ZETTEL*. Edited by G.E.M Anscombe & G.H. von Wright.
     Translated by G.E.M. Anscombe. University of California Press, 1967.

"Consoling System" was written in 2012 with no particular president in mind but rather the abstract idea of the president as "national consoler."

"Simultaneously" and "Proper Expressions of Love" are for John. Thank you for loving me through it.

For Etta.

Acknowledgments

Grateful acknowledgment to the editors of the following journals where these poems were first published, sometimes in different forms.

Alaska Quarterly Review: "Prepositions Against Desire"
A Public Space: "Consoling System"
Arroyo Literary Review: "System of Knowing," "System with Some Truth"
Blackbird: "How We Take Our Grief"
The Collapsar: "A Difficult System," "Postmodern Dirge"
Fourteen Hills: "Family System"
Grist: A Journal of the Literary Arts: "We Were Civilized When?"
The Harlequin: "System for After"
jubilat: "A System of Holding"
Linebreak: "No System for Grief"
Lit Magazine: "Simultaneously"
Narrative Magazine: "The Mercy of Pronouns," "Unsystem the System"
On the Seawall: "Interview with Anne Carson," "Interview with Gertrude Stein"
The Rumpus: "Love in the Time of Formlessness (or Form in the Time of Lovelessness)"
The Paris-American: "Rhetoric," "Reason"
Tin House: "System of Becoming Quite"

"A System of Holding" was republished on *Verse Daily*.

This book was written with the gracious support of Stanford University, the Civitella Ranieri Foundation, the University of Cincinnati, and the Lexi Rudnitsky Poetry Project.

Thank you, Gabriel Fried, editor extraordinaire.